A HEART OF INK

A Journey From Darkness to Understanding

Coral T. Hahn

DEDICATION

I dedicate this book to my beloved Lord and Savior Jesus Christ, whose love surpasses that of human love and who has kept His promises, to my mother, who long ago encouraged me to make an illustrated poetry book, to brothers in Christ in my past who inspired me with their perseverance, gentleness, friendship and love of Truth and to ministry partners who deeply touched and changed my life.

To those who stood in my corner through the publication process: Susan, Raul, Alex, Chris and End Times Productions, my agent and the publisher who truly encouraged me to keep hold of my faith in my Lord and to keep hoping for the best.

A Heart of Ink
by Coral Tulle Hahn
Copyright ©2020 Coral Tulle Hahn

ISBN 978-1-951561-14-7 (print)
ISBN 978-1-951561-15-4 (ebook)
For Worldwide Distribution
Printed in the U.S.A.

River Birch Press
P.O. Box 868, Daphne, AL 36526

CONTENTS

Cold Loneliness   *1*

Gentleness   *3*

Poem of a Warrior   *5*

The Boy That Drove Me Crazy   *7*

So Close, So Far   *9*

Ghostly Places   *11*

Doubting Lane   *13*

My Wish   *15*

Dreaming of My First Kiss   *17*

God   *19*

My High Perch   *21*

Winter in the Heart   *23*

Hollow   *25*

On Hands and Knees   *27*

All Things Possible   *29*

Depthless   *31*

Love Reflections   *33*

Leaf Under the Tree   *34*

House of Treasures   *36*

When I Skate   *39*

Bullets and Butterflies   *41*

Unwantables   *42*

Resting on His Paws   *45*

Truth   *47*

Filled   *49*

Grateful Tears   *51*

First Autumn Morning   *53*

The Whisperer   *55*

Celebration by Myself   *57*

Amazing Grace Sheep   *58*

Cling to the Twig   *61*

Privileged Ear   *63*

Birth of a Soul   *65*

Bunny   *67*

Jasmine on the Wall   *68*

Outside the Church, Outside the Steeple:
    Poem Under Construction   *70*

Shoosh   *72*

Tears on Throned Steps   *75*

Traveler's Poem   *77*

Heart of Spring   *79*

The Moon Rose   *81*

Gate of Love   *83*

Sky in the Night   *85*

Musical Love   *87*

Language of the Wind   *89*

A Heart of Ink   *91*

COLD LONELINESS

Cold are the winds and gales of life,
Reality shows me how to go.
Mourning life around me,
Lonely am I on this one person journey.
Trying to fend for myself,
Loneliness made worse by the knowing,
You believe in me,
You care for me,
So far away.
The sweet imagination in my head,
Creates a different story.
One where I have you by my side
To hold and be held by in comfort.
Your care and heart's smile,
In my memory,
Smears the gray,
Revealing hints of gold, pink, and peach.
Morning in the heart.
My hope to see you soon,
Mourning in my feet
That travel on.

GENTLENESS

I feel the sun, so warm.
Reminds me of love.
Love exists in the world!
The joy of a smile, so sweet.
Reminds me of happiness
Bubbling over about you.
The hug of warmth,
The expression of joy.
Have decided to give you
The chance to keep up.
Love exists in the world!
Remind me to wait
For good relationships.
Shun rush, welcome trust.
Even though far away,
I believe
That you care for me.

POEM OF A WARRIOR

Ancient Enemy of past,
Rises in my dreams.
Battle during the night,
Fears that persist,
That want to claim me,
Make me believe them.
Present battle of jealousy,
Of being stuck here in my time.
Demons of my
Selfishness and independence
In the shadows track me.
Warriors are lonely folk,
For no one wants to be them.
We are always there for others,
Whether in prayer or comfort.
But sigh, doing battle all the time,
Strengthens and weakens me.
Ready for the next one,
I know I can win,
The arrow will miss me.

THE BOY THAT DROVE
ME CRAZY

Boy, you drive me crazy.
Crazy in great ways.
The distance seemed so small,
So big when I thought of you,
The crazy times we had.
Talking on the phone
In early hours till night.
Boy, you drive me crazy,
Crazy in bitter ways.
The distance increased as time went by.
I never heard from you.
How I wanted you to come for me.
Talk and share the happiness
In those crazy times
Again that we once had.
I miss your smile,
Your gentle look.
Feeling secure in a dying flame,
And knowing you were there.
Will it be so?
Will it be so?
Was it ever so?
Answer: No.

SO CLOSE, SO FAR

The canyon walls echo
Only with lonely jays.
Beside the redwoods,
I feel so small and far away.
Everywhere I go I miss you,
Even on the cliffs at night.
Watching the waves and fog roll in,
Covering the many promises of visits.
Wishing you there to keep me warm and close.
Everywhere I go I miss your charming heart.
Hand in hand in my mind,
I walk beside you through forest.
In fantastical time
I want for you to come,
But your absence keeps me company.
I feel I am too needy.
Yet, is this what our Maker wants for us?
I want to know you love me too!
But if you don't,
Somehow I'll make it through.
Sad and crying,
I await your appearance in vain.
Would that we could walk side by side again.

GHOSTLY PLACES

Walking across a memory of green,
One gazes in awe at sun-filled sky.
At an evening of communion,
Between God and you in a starry night.
Standing on a carpet of a four-year home,
Your brothers, sisters, and friends well known,
Played in the kingdom nursery where
We had so much fun growing.
Visiting the sanctuary that seems so small,
Yet held all His children.
There, I gave my pledge to grow.
Yet, humble my heart as a servant.
Wise men travelled far to teach us
What God desires us to show others.
In amongst the cabins,
Memories like ghosts

Fly in the breeze.
Giggles of times shared,
Inside jokes, crushes, having fun
In an upright environment.
Having left, yet coming back,
One sees the people or events
That makes each slab of stone,
Each flower,
Each conversation,
Important and historic.
Having graduated,
Yet letting the blessing soak in.
One can decide to come back
To this wonderful ground and bless it—
Creating more memories
To joyfully haunt other kingdom kin.

DOUBTING LANE

In the past I've been tricked
By verbal scandal,
And by winks or words of hollow joy.
I have been pricked.
Down the lane of doubt,
My mind travels
When you act so generous,
Loving and full of kindness.
Been corrupted before,
Or led on by silly foolishness.
With you, love seems a different thing.
I hope you follow God first,
Although my heart wants to cling.
Doubt, distrust, distress are ever
In the back of my mind.
When you say I am a gem
Or how much you care,

The more I feel comfortable to share.
We are great friends.
I want God to lead.
I gave up following men
Who call themselves a stag or steed.
As much as this feels correct, honest, and right,
My mind seems still
To have doubt I wish I could fight.
The stories of loves across a continent,
Waiting faithfully for
The other's return,
Being so in tune,
As to memorize the other in their head.
Only God loves supremely,
But I travel the doubting lane
And found it true,
That you no longer love me some degree too.

MY WISH

My wish is simple.
It comes from a place
Of utmost comfort.
A wish to have a companion
Wells up in me
These cold winter days,
While watching snowflakes and TV.
Doing homework,
Listening to music
That will stem my imagination,
And atop the dreamy dandelion,
My wish is to see
What wonderful guy awaits.
To talk to,

When sad or tired,
Lean on each other's back,
To have more times of unseparated friendship.
My wish is to run in the woods with you.
To catch a dandelion.
And make each other's dreams come true.
To be wrapped in admiration, comfort, and love.
To have permission to embrace you.
To share godly pride in joy.
To know respect and safe ambience
When we are beside.
To laugh and twirl,
Around and around.
Dizzy, celebrating round the King's crown.

DREAMING OF MY FIRST KISS

Cannot imagine sweetness
Without the sense of taste.
Cannot imagine beauty
Without the sense of character.
Cannot imagine the kiss
I dream of having from you.
Can dream of the bliss, the joy.
Can imagine how it might be,
Though I cannot begin to try.
Can put you, not me, first.
Cannot accept what you say
Conflicting with your thought.
Will wait to feel gently caught.
Will hope for the wonderful feeling
Walking beside you will bless.
Can wait for love to grow.
Can be sure I love you even now.
Will wait for the kiss
At the altar someday.

GOD

God fills me with indescribable joy.
God leads me on this path.
On my own,
Things wind around me in confusion.
God knows me and waits for me
To follow Him.
God makes me look around life
At all His inspiration.
On my own,
I sit in contemplation.
God comforts me
That good things are to come,
And hugs me when life
Goes up in consternation.
On my own,
I think of my future.
God tells my heart,
"Don't worry"
God knows what will be.
On my own,
I sit in growing trust of Him,
Who knows my wishes and my needs,
As once again,
I hand them over to Him.

MY HIGH PERCH

In my high perch,
Memories of the past
Warm my heart,
As in my cozy place,
I look down upon it.
The big house my friend had,
And how we used to chase the cats.
When I looked out,
The golden hills all around.
The memories—
I look down into the past.
How, from another high place,
As a child,
Being twirled in the air
Like a plane once.

The memory—
I look down
Into the cool, pleasant night,
With two people in love
By a clear fountain lighted.
These are just some
Memories that make
Me happy
As I seek the highest place
That I can take.
To look back and down
On happy memories,
Making my soul
Cozy, safe, and at ease.

WINTER IN THE HEART

Listening to the notes on the freezing wind,
I walk in the snowy land of my epitaph.
My heart asunder looking for a reason,
Listening to the tune of my wandering spirit,
Listening for the reason my life is so cold.
Without the people who love me,
Studying my past,
Not really depressed.
But, in the deep state of aloneness,
Feeling the snow.
Remembering how my life is so cold.
Without the people who love me,
But will never from that love receive.
So estranged, so lonely I look.
Standing, looking for a reason for warmth.
Head cocked toward the sky.
Eyes closed.
Yet, I can see the icicle tears
I am not even let to cry.
So cold being alive and dead,
Feeling estranged in familiar land,
Haunted by happy visions
Of my past that I run for,
Which dissipate into the snowy bank
And I realize they are mirages.
Is there a way out of this land?
The land of epitaph—

Where I feel so cold when alive,
Knowing there are little glows in the distance?
Cold creeps into my face, fingers, toes, and feet,
Till I cannot feel anything
Except bitterness' enveloping sting.
Listening for the voices on the wind,
From friend afar.
I start to run toward the gates,
But tying bonds of ice are too strong.
I will stay, uncomforted by anything,
Except for the knowledge that my self-sacrifice
May someday come to some worth.
Listening, leaning on the tree,
Snowflakes float around my face,
Presenting through all the turmoil:
A young beauty full of grace.
Though I struggle through this land,
Of constant cold
And nothing,
But memories and misunderstandings.
I know I have the power to call upon
The warmth from the deep inside me.
All my wishes are put to an end,
As I stand resolute, meek, and confident.
Searching for warmth from inside
That will melt the snows away.

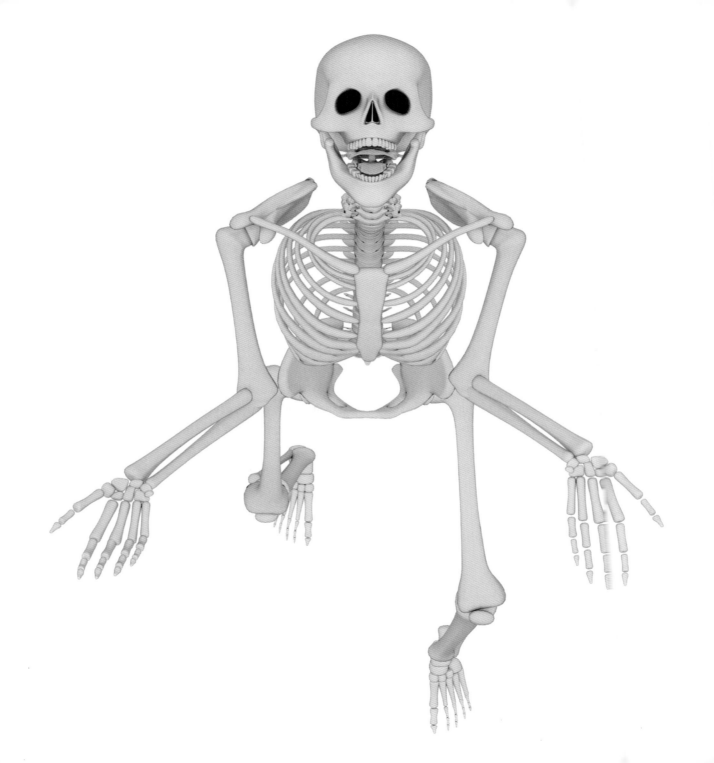

HOLLOW

The old man's eyes so hollow, given up.
Picked his battle to fix others,
His experience with God is moved on.
His identity lost.
The dreams of heavenly goals nigh dead.
Never got what he wanted in life,
Never really told anybody.
Unadmittant to living in a grave,
His eyes peer out of skulled skeleton of soul
    so hollow!
Consumed by all the lost desires,
He hides behind nothing,
Not knowing he is seen.
Not allowing others to obtain what they love,
Never giving a reason for guidelines and belief.
Hollow eyes, so starving
For what people cannot give.
Thus he sits within Creator's sight,
With no life.

Away from what could surround him.
Such a hollow life
That threatens so to crumble,
Clings a skeleton to pride.
Hollow eyes, be filled.
See the world from a different perspective!
With knowledge and admission listen,
Or you might be left behind.
Mortality is not everlasting.
Hollow eyes,
A beggar,
By the monochrome, empty road,
Refusing to surrender to God's plan.
Striking out while crying "Alms"
With bitterness and sarcasm.
So I bow now, kneel, and pray,
For hollow eyes to be no more
Like an empty filled grave.

ON HANDS AND KNEES

What to write about?
Too long I've been gone.
Too long I've been asleep.
Too long I've felt separated
By work from calm and peace.
No nights, no days.
Exhaustion in heart, mind, and body phase.
How much missing loved ones
Does missing cost?
Too much of anything.
Lord, I feel the loss.

ALL THINGS POSSIBLE

Spunky child,
Skipping by His side,
Holding onto His hand,
Along with the friends
Who are children in the faith.
Following His footsteps,
Gazing in wonder,
At His gentle, beaming, joyful face.
He lifts me up to touch the stars.
He gives us all voices of praise.
The great Creator,
So that we can ride on wings like eagles,
Racing over the heavens,
Listening and singing with glee!
It is so vast!
Nothing contained, so bright!
Yet, His riches and provision
Shine so particularly.
No one might look like they did on earth,
But you know them

Because they remain kindred spirits,
And you make the connection.
We walk alongside,
Some learning to stand by,
Holding onto His robe
As He walks us through our tough times.
By telling us parables,
And calling our names.
Guiding us through life's journey
Because He knows the way.
He has been there and elsewhere,
Many times before.
We follow Him,
Seeing His miracles
Deeper appreciating His love.
So overflowed with
The joy of Heaven coming,
We dance toward the finish line
Of a forever beginning.

DEPTHLESS

Such a little cup I hold,
Yet, the love surrounding me—
It's what makes this moment possible.
So small an object,
That moves me so to tears,
Because I know my shame.
From sins thought,
And ones not known,
To come through the years.
Such a depthless cup,
So small I hold in my hand,
While my spirit beams
Of the victory found in forgiveness.
I drink of the waterfalls of His voice,
That bled blood red,
And in white,
Purified my soul from falling.
Such a depthless moment
In a precious little building.
His love pours into my soul,
Through the wine, the pact.
His life He gave for me.
Within my tent, glowing with joy and peace
My heart hears the words:
"I love you. I love you. Remember Me."

LOVE REFLECTIONS

Your love reflects a future dream.
Just as the sunrise
Through the clouds,
Show upon the windows.
God's grace and gentle nature
Comes to me
Through His voice,
Through His creation.
The way I hope to be loved,
Respected and cherished by a man,
Makes me miss him,
Even though I've not yet met him.
However, the knowledge
Of our friendship, our love,
Makes me wait
Patiently and joyfully.
Wait to look you in the eye.
Wait for you to look into mine,
See the Almighty living in ourselves.
To someday soon
See a bright, beautiful sunrise,
To see love no longer waiting
In each other's eyes.

LEAF UNDER THE TREE

The beaten, ancient tree
Sheds her soft, golden, red and tan tears
For the season that is just beginning.
Announces that the summer is over.
Last night I contentedly fell asleep.
Fond memories with joy,
I was by your side and you beamed.

God wraps me with
That warm, loved knowing
You could not provide.
That blessed knowledge,
That through these
Falling seasons of my life,
He will always bring

Those needed to come alongside.
Binding us all,
In the special collection of fall.
Colors and shapes that He gathers.
So we will be
Together for eternity.
Gone a season,
Will see each dear person,
Yet again,
Under the ancient tree.
Though one person,
One leaf right now,
Occupies a good portion of the mind,
Other precious leaves as well
Take up mind's time:
The one who looks needy,
The one who looks tired
And struggles most of the time.
The one who hides
The pain behind their cheer.
But don't worry, leaves,
I am always near in prayer.
The One whom no one can discourage.
Oh, would it be joyful times
To converse with these again
To warn you about life as well as jest.
The one who acts perverted, lost his way,
Needing something called a godly path,

Chided and wiser someday.
The one who has gained joy
In having love from
The ones who look so sad.
My prayer is for you
To be there for each other,
In the reconciling, you once had.
Sit under the ancient.
Walk around the circle.
Tread the myriad of leaves.
The precious colors,
Faces have lighted up my life.
How many leaves God has inspired
To take courage and someday congregate?
A season must pass,
Where friends fall,
So keep touch until that time.
A commodity I will be so glad to share
Dear friends of mine,
Who speak God's truth and let it shine
In order to see things glanced over before.
See their needs?
In their eyes?
These leaves under the tree?
So again there I will see you, hopefully.
Gathered by the One
Who was hung upon the ancient's beam.

HOUSE OF TREASURES

Wake up from a sound night's sleep,
Full of pleasant, soothing dreams
Of happiness and joy—
Such as chasing feathers or butterflies.
Slide down an ice cream castle,
Bite the cherry on top.
Wake up again,
In the morning light,
Calling you forth
To start the new day
That will be full of
New things, new surprises.
Toes reach down
As you get out of the feather-soft bed
To pleasantly squish into a carpet
That was made from clouds.

Force open the door
To a brand-new day,
Fighting the wind from
The AC holding it shut.
Say hello to the ladybugs
Painted beside upon the switch.
Dance with the rainbows
That glitter and move in the hallway,
Refracted off the crystal door-glass
On the mirror, couch, and floorboards,
Counting each one before breakfast:
A hearty meal, full of sweetness—
Juice of the pears and apples, plucked fresh.
Bananas in a bowl of milk,
And blueberry muffins caked
With clumps of sugar on top.
First eaten because of its crunchiness.
The day holds many adventures.
Play a game running round the yard.
Stare at the statue of the otter by the pool.
Run and put an ice cube in the water wheel.
Breathe deeply the aroma of the calla lilies.
Run through the weather-nurtured grass
Like the bees that fly in circles,
After drinking profoundly of the
Pollen of the peace roses.
Be Grandpa's little assistant in the garden—
Wrestling lemons, peaches from the trees.

Dive into water clear as the Caribbean.
Throw down rocks
To the bottom of the jacuzzi.
Later enjoy the gathering of dinner.
Watch as a spread of yellow and red
Soften the evening sky,
Transitioning to peach, pink, and lavender,
Light to dark blue
And beyond that—black.
The doggie is put to bed
And the TV turned off.
The stars above this peaceful house
Say it's time for bed.
You silently say goodnight
To the garden, the pool,
The piano, chairs, and rugs.
How sad to go to sleep,
But remember the fluffy, safe bed!
There is always tomorrow
To raid the cookie jar!
To run in the grass,
And smile and the clear blue sky.
Reading from Grandpa's bookshelf
Next to the warmth of the hearth.
So it is every time
I come back to this house.
Feeling welcome to its hidden treasures.

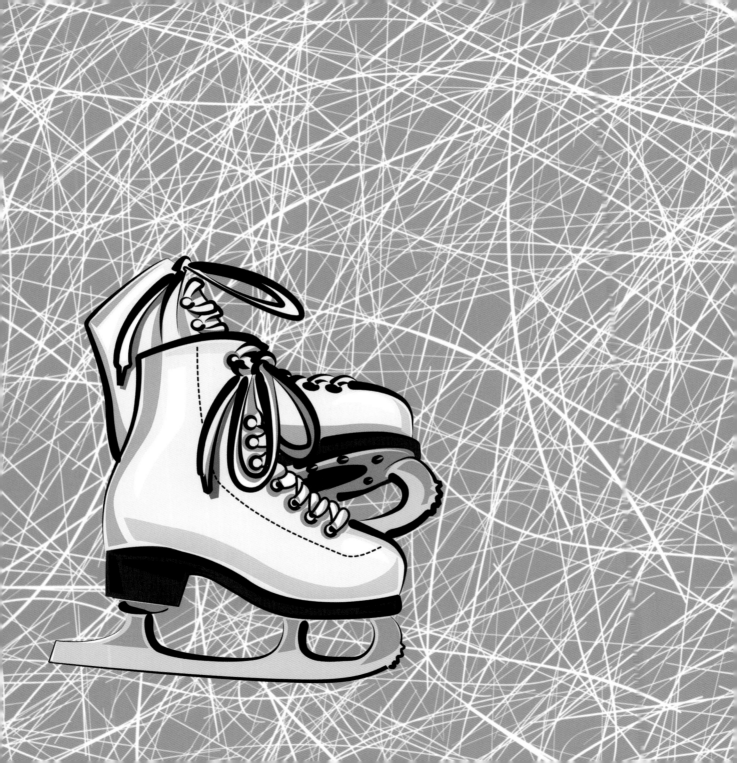

WHEN I SKATE

When I skate
In my own little world,
I can turn the lights on dim,
Or bright as day.
Recreate places I have been,
My own environment.
Sometimes of a tribal flavor,
Or perhaps another culture.
I know this dance,
It is a comfort to the heart.
To skate,
Feeling graceful,
In my imagination.
Music on the speakers loud.
I am in a place,
More beautiful than here.
To forget the
Confusion of my mind,
Free and peaceful.
Fulfilled by the wind in the hair
When one flies by.

Inner balance and strength
As one latches onto creativity's trail.
No human to judge you,
Expression complete.
Air suspending your gravity.
What a pity the music has to end,
Since these times of skating alone
Are like little bits of heaven on earth.
Giving thanks, and expressing
Love to the Creator,
I find such joy and triumph.
A place where I can soar, glide.
A place to find strength
From above, from inside.
My dreams come true here,
And as the music ends,
I sit on the ice,
Close my eyes,
Breathe deeply,
Letting the cold joy soak
Into my soul completely.

BULLETS AND BUTTERFLIES

A bridge of friendly fellowship,
Butterfly of attraction,
Its wings unfold,
Sweet and protective,
Yet unrequited.
Sadly understanding.
A story dies before beginning.
Chance could not stand,
For another unknown awaits.
Recipient's heart
Refuses to turn truth into a lie,
Even though chivalry
Humbly requested a kiss.
A kiss denied.
Bullets shoot through woven wings.

Wincing, the shooter
Blesses life and healing.
Heal, heal, flutterer,
Sad and shy.
The moment fades.
Lessons taught, cherished, unforgotten.
Watched the healing.
Heart loved by
Someone who became the best.
Making the offered smile, blessed.
Healed heart
At the foot of the Cross
With the companion
With which they were designed.

UNWANTABLES

Some people are ghosts of the present,
Unaware of the presence of the shunned.
The ones who live day to day
In emptiness, fake externalness,

Growing not, interact in the dumb.
Seeing not outside of self,
Seeing not the lonely creep,
Who has the lisp or bad eye,

42

Stereotype, hated for something
Not their fault.
The skinny "jerk"
Who became so through
The cruel trick
Of sophisticated tactics,
Then thrown from the circle.
Laughed at for being a square or octagon.
My heart breaks for these unwantables
Since I am turning into one of them.
This dangerous clique I left
Seems so unreacheable,
Just filling my soul with frustration.
I will go to those who want an ear.
The others will get the hell they bear.
In the future only to be faces
To their past realizations.
But you, you are different, unwantable!
You brought a smile to my soul
When inside is seen the tears you hold
Within countenance's shell.
Someone patted me on the shoulder,
    affirming me.
When I needed someone to talk to,
So I give to you too!
Your genuine heart shone through.
Taught me further attentiveness of ear
Of things to come.

So do I turn you to the One!
Hope held in sharing my conviction,
You find all that your heart
Has desired and hoped for—
Mystery unlocked,
Yet deeper—the Gospel.
God to me. Me to you.
"That is the Gospel truth"
Sharing His blood and
My honest experience of testimony.
The unwantables.
Honesty. Love. Belief unfaçaded.
Prayer of truth's recognition
To make this more a world of smiles!
Bless the unwantables,
To see and be life in and as
Your humble servants.
The gentle Spirit that abides,
Succeeding in life,
Walking in true wisdom, light, and love.
Take away the guns, blades, and drugs,
Hate of self and others unjustly judged.
Pat someone on the back.
Listen to their joys and tears.
Treat them as precious,
Because we ourselves believe
In the LIVING God.

RESTING ON HIS PAWS

Exhaustion, peace, and soothing,
Call my head to lay between Holy paws.
Relying on the promise of rest
Amidst turmoil.
Calm.
Relaxing.
I fall asleep,
To thoughts that bring a smile.
Holy paws invite to ponder,
How wonderful heaven will be.
Safe and secure in the indestructible,
I close my eyes and fall asleep.

TRUTH

Why is it so hard to speak the truth?
So hard to share God's love?
Why and how can they reject the sun,
And hide the good inside?
They work so tirelessly quilting
The blanket of ignorance and excuse!
The challenge, the quest for me,
Has not yet come to be over.
Can I be what God wants me to be?
Can I penetrate the stone walls
That rise so high
With the simple warmth
Of His love?
When I consider giving up
And walking away,
God inspires me.

Sending amazing friends
Who pick me up along with Him.
Encouraging me to faith unshunned,
To glow—piercing the shades,
The dark covers.
Penetrate the holes left by the needle,
Much like starshine in the heavens.
Light calls through the soulful night.
He seeks to love,
To catch a glimpse of reflected glory.
To never be afraid to live
And speak out truth.
So are they who want to escape hell's lion
Who seeks to hold them captive,
Gaping wide his bloody teeth.

FILLED

The sunset is what happens
When God chugs paint
Into the realms,
To fill it with
Unique combination
Of color to remind us
Of love's vastness.
The cross is what happened
When God sent His Beloved,
To overcome death and sin.
Why do we think
We can be filled
With passing lustful attraction?
When did the believer abandon
The full sense of love in his heart?
The home to hope and peace,
To settle content,
Easily fit in
With culture's grace—
Away from "Thou Art,"
How long has it been
Since you who read the word,
Read with understanding,
Have known the all secure
Full-measure of Christ's love,

Just as when you wake
To life of a cold morning?
The warmth of favorite blanket preferring?
Has anyone told you how wonderful feeling,
Fulfilled with the injection of the nail,
How Christ has had our pain,
All sorrow through Him,
Created everything in creation,
"Today you will be with me in paradise"
Comes to mind of the thief on the cross.
Repetitive preaching
Has pounded Salvation's helmet.
His birth and our necessary rebirth
Has been untaught
By the satisfaction of creation.
Like a child
Many jump up and down,
Claiming attention
To our worthy desires
So His beaming face
Will give us hope, joy, and crown.
The knowledge of fullness
Of the warmth of salvation or love—
You CAN BE filled,
Just keep looking to Him alone—above.

GRATEFUL TEARS

Have you ever heard
A beautiful song,
Sung by a fellow soul
Of the heavenly crown?
So beautiful are the lyrics,
Holding powerful truth,
That you cry with grateful tears,
That you were saved
When you were
To hear such notes?

I have heard such a song.
God granted me to listen,
And I heard and felt
The same love
When I was first claimed by Him.
How unspeakably wonderful
His presence of love and forgiveness is,
When it makes you cry with gladness.
Being once again assured
That in your own dark hour of life,
He holds the reason of everything.
You'll not be abandoned.

FIRST AUTUMN MORNING

I get through reading my Bible,
Routine in the morning.
I stretch,
Looking out the window.
Everything looks the same.
The sunlight from the east
Caresses the backyard bushes,
Creating a lovely pattern of gold
And gentle shadows in the woods.
But something is different.
My body senses.
I look at the row of apples
On the windowsill.
Suddenly, recognition of the chill,
Of the breath of the season.
The joys of harvest time.
The apples from the orchard.
Sweet cider and maple syrup treats.
The indescribable awe

Of how God cloaks the trees.
Yellows, browns, purples, oranges, and reds.
The simple love of curling up
In a blanket warm
During the chilly nights.
Awakening in the morning
To disturb the silver-coated grasses.
The warmth of the sun, more noticeable.
So, throw more logs upon
The fire in the fireplace!
The season is like the last
Of the ripe fruits.
Rides on farms,
The smell of hay,
Are memories of autumns past.
The first morning of autumn
Has come at long last!
Hurrah, hurray!

THE WHISPERER

He comes so subtle,
Slightly breathing thoughts unfit.
His favorite hobbies
Involve trying to get the faithful
To stumble in their flesh.
The weaker to fall,
His black rule is deceit.
He lives in the pit.
Some make him out
To be a cartoon.
They underestimate
His capability of influence,
Just like he wants them to think.
He likes grabbing
The living's attention,
Influencing them to be
Puffed up and worship him.
Dwelling on the past,
Hopelessness, and even recent sins.
But, as the whisperer comes,

You ought to know his tactics.
The one thing he doesn't want you to know,
Is that he can be defeated.
That your heart, soul, and mind
Is Christ's,
When you gave them
To their Creator.
Respond with authority.
Learn His vs. your righteousness.
You recognize the whispers
That seek to destroy you,
Brothers, sisters.
Pay no credence and rebuke.
Dwell instead on thoughts
Implanted by the Spirit!
Never forget
To call on Christ
To fight for you
For His strength is perfect
And He is victorious!

CELEBRATION BY MYSELF

See me.
See me eat.
See me eat the chocolate muffin!
See me dance very happily!
See me get extremely silly!
See me celebrate by myself.
See my joy as I put on music.
See me get dizzy.
See me giggle at myself.
These are things that go unseen
By other folks!

AMAZING GRACE SHEEP

The little lamb will follow,
Not looking back,
But follows through the valley
Of the shadow of death.
This world.
This spiritual realm.
She dedicated all to the Shepherd,
Including her love of man.
Not knowing what to expect.
Her Shepherd leads her
To face trials yet.
But even though many voices
Whisper through the hills,
The Shepherd is right
Beside the sheep
And smiles,
Saying, "Peace, be still."

She knows this journey is for her,
Despite that which she cannot see.
The blinders from the predators
Are for her protection.
She knows in her soul
The Master is near,
Drawing out her inner fear.
Through street and field,
She will follow,
Hoping for that rich, green fallow.
Faith by hope,
Not by sight alone,
Proceeds by poetry
From things He places
In her head at night,
Lying down, safe and secure.
He plays the harp and sings for her.

She loves His robe, His feet,
And the gentle presence.
She lays her sheep head
On His feet in reverence.
She rustles.
He scratches her ears.
"Don't worry, little one.
They do not dare, no matter how near.
I am nearer.
I am omnipotent.
I can protect you from all the lies.
I love your steadfastness,
Even when you near the brink.
You bleat out to Me,
And find I am beside you in a wink.
I am inside you, beside.
Don't worry, My little sheep.
I see.
You see through My eyes—
All the deadness.
You will someday be a strong sheep,
My sweet, little lamb.
In the valley of the shadow is this world.
You see the souls
Who believe they are living.
But even within this, My flock,
Death claims them
Who trade truth for lies

So you bleat out your love for Me.
Do not give up to try."
Oh, how I love you Jesus.
I love being your sheep.
Writing, talking to you
Within myself—
Pure love—content.
Together, me following You,
I shall make it.
I pray for the entire herd:
Saints, warriors, prophets, and ministers.
It gets easier. It gets harder.
Yes, the days draw near.
But though I am a lamby sheep,
I know El Shaddai
Will come soon to reap.
I grow and rest
In the valley of wolves and bones.
The GOOD Shepherd keeps me safe,
Though seeming to tarry long.
One day I will have a bright, white robe
And see my soul.
I never have.
Someday along the horizon soon,
He will come and claim me.
Healing and restoration
Will come by living fountain.
I will be free from this tent and be made whole!

CLING TO THE TWIG

When in the midst of the dark,
And under attack.
When faith is the mark,
Pray for help and hope to above.
Cling,
Cling to the twig.

When the Enemy laughs,
And you are hedged in.
When depressed, cry out.
Or make a call for fellowship.
Cling,
Cling to the twig.

When on the mountain.
When doused in the downpour of His love.
Raise it on high!
Cling,
Cling to the branch.

When brought before the tree,
In shame of past or present

And facing condemnation
One cannot handle by self
And humbled.
Look down at your hand
And remember who you are in Him.
Cling,
Cling to the branch.

When just walking in latter days,
The long and narrow road.
And none will follow, even when you age.
It seems so long!
Cling,
Cling to the wood in hand.

When you reach heaven's gate,
And are overwhelmed.
Clench the fist and discover
The twig has grown
Into a companion through it all
A leaning post,
A walking stick.

PRIVILEGED EAR

A gift of human friend,
A beloved young man
Whom I dearly admired.
His renewed life I heard
Beating, thriving,
As a symbol of life
Deep within his chest.
He took my head,
And securely enfolded it
Close to his earthly shell.
I felt so secure,
Treasured, protected.
My privileged ear heard
And loved his heartbeat.
Steady, strong it throbbed.
And I could sense
A love that emanated.

A love for me.
I feel at peace.
Joyful that I had such a treasured space.
My privileged ear longs
For such a gentle place
With the one Abba has in mind.
A sound unlike any other.
Comforting, makes me smile
Through my tears.
The privilege since
Has long gone away.
Yet, still I hope of such rest again
With whose love in Him
Strives not to fail,
Though we may
Stumble and disappoint
As we are beings.

BIRTH OF A SOUL

I came up out of water
And of Holy Fire unseen.
Still the same
In appearance outward.
Still by my name on earth.
Yet some indescribable thing
Foretelling me
As I walked to the waves,
Hoping I would be different
Made anew by the One Who saves.

I dipped down into a watery cemetery
All was gritty, dark, and salt.
Entered my ears, eyes, nose, and mouth.
My spirit had a long moment in darkness
I died there.
My old sin and everything

That was in my dead and torn tent
Washed away with the tide.
I cried out inaudible to physical ears
And wholesome Spirit filled my being
With new life to live for the One
Who became one with me.
I had heard and learnt about
But now know personally, deeply.

I am lifted from the water
And amidst the celebration
I am not freezing
Though it is late August.
My body feels wrapped
With soft fire that refuses to depart
A warmth around myself
A heavenly blanket.

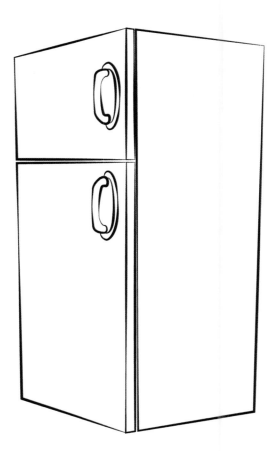

BUNNY

Thump!
Hours of unending wakefulness,
Staring at the ceiling.
Rustling newspapers,
I hear bunnies pacing.
Slowly verging
On the border
To the land of sleep…

THUMP!
Is the reply,
Sending my heart to shock.
And my brain realizing,
Once again,
The warm summer night.

"GO TO SLEEP!"
I wail inside.
The refridge is bothering them,
You see,
Since it was moved slightly to the side!

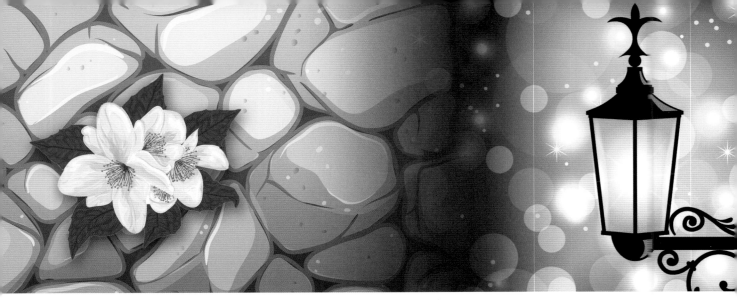

JASMINE ON THE WALL

The wall you see in my eyes
The midnight blue
Of Springtime's kind
Night atmosphere.
Wafts of jasmine soft
Complimented by the
Station light's glow.
Your eyes seen clearly
Through your glasses.
The single, starry light shines
On the night sky
Around your pupils.
Like a last faint glimmer
Of hope, when before
They held galaxies of dreams.
The refined blue of the daytime

Surrounded the depths that widened
In days of a heart's rich wonder
Are royal blue as when the skies
Threaten storm and rain
Wanting to rend me
With the thunders of your angry pain.
That momentary evening
My prayers I thought answered
In the rain gently showering down.
In the world where our hearts spoke
In the darkness before.
I didn't see how you couldn't
See, hear, or sense.
A wall you say you see,
A wall around my heart.
Of this you are right

The stones should be familiar.
Some you placed there.
I listened,
Singing hope inside,
That you'd recognize my heart's song.
That you'd actually hear my prayers.
Excuses and desires drown any song.
Yet that evening I still sang, hoping
That you not get tired
Journeying around the garden wall
For the gate more precious
Than the physical.
Not to give up upon your
Vast treasure awaiting inside
Once so fought for.
To pick up the crown
Cast away by your hand.
Of finding the gate
To my heart to guard it.
Singing for your ears to be opened
To my prayers not said aloud,
Once understood looking into my eyes.
Singing for your understanding to be opened.
But the evening sits still.
The wafts of jasmine stop twirling.
The station where we stood
A faded picture left there.
In time and space away.

So much greatness intended.
Some love the thrill of emotion's roller coaster,
Some call love a game,
Some seek out the long and steady,
Courageous, sacrificial life of strengthening.
Promises unseen have a cost.
Forgetfulness as well that God
Made us strong to compliment.
But hands let go
And so
Upon the windy way of faults stripped,
The fight of faith becomes unknit.
There yet are parts of each other's
Heart land not yet known.
Paths of His plan not yet trod.
Song ceases from the soft and delicate part
Of this hard-edged warrior's heart.
Seen in part—
Just a part is not everything.
I am to show someone else my world
Who will turn the key
Who will enter and stay
Such unending, wonderfully unfolding Eden.
Here our melodies must part
Beneath the lighted lamp
With nothing but the pavement
And jasmine on which to glow.

OUTSIDE THE CHURCH, OUTSIDE THE STEEPLE: POEM UNDER CONSTRUCTION

There is the church.
There is the steeple.
I stand outside,
Yet I'm one of the kingdom's people.
My soul artistic,
Saved by the King.
Blessing bestowed,
Yet hard understood.
Such as "blessed are your eyes
For others longed but did not"
Blessing on being ostracized
Because of His name.
By the legitimate
Soul lineage of the King,
The mustard seeds
Dance, shout, and sing.
The houses of God
Wear away to silos
Stored in silence
Of things truly believed.
In the vastness,
Some still build altars of prayers
Made of stones
To show what they hope
More hearts won't become.
Souls who,
Like lamps wreathed in incense,
See the highways and hedges
Along His path.

Houses are designed for family,
Though not everyone will choose.
Too much opportunity of love is lost.
Proof through history and talkative,
    debatable sort.
Except life and faith,
Themselves reflected and appreciated.
Again and again, so weary a road,
So many kept at arms-length,
Never knowing,
Save beyond
Manmade logistics and ultimatums.
Outside the church.
Outside the steeple.
Outside of comfort and into strength
Via discipline and courage.
Who will open the doors
Since workers and the family-less are knocking?
More workers are needed.
Just outside of the church.
Just outside the steeple.
Souls starving
For truth, love, joy, peace,
Comfort, edification.
Beings named people.
But the treasury of mustard seeds
Refuses and stays within.
This poem though, perhaps,
Is still under construction.

SHOOSH

Heart with
Hardly blood to pump,
Gaping wide
With bullet holes.
"Shoosh,"
They sing
As they zing
From the trigger
Of people who know not,
Or who have

Gone through the same
Who should know
Somewhat better.
Imagine.
Imagine the sound
Of lead tearing flesh.
Open your ears.
Don't you close your eyes.
I will write the sounds
For each having felt this.

Your tongue
Is responsible:
Bringing life or death.
People's words,
Too many have caused
To be like this.
Rupturing, spewing,
Gaping wide holes.
And so another heart goes.
Holes of slander.
Holes of malice.
Holes of hatred.
Holes of loved ones joined to.
Holes of negligence.
"Shoosh,"
Hearts are told.
"I've been there too."
Words that seem
Older and wiser, yet cruel.
Cruelly, unspecifically explained.
Cruelly declared as just.
People will shoot you.
"Don't let your dying breath
Be your excuse.
Don't be sad.
Only focus on
What should make you glad.
Joy will give you strength."

Ignoring the holes
In others and themselves,
Nothing succeeds.
Life once so fluent
Slowly recedes.
It all comes down
To a single muscle:
Flesh and sinew.
Still and silent,
Nothing left that's held.
Nothing considered sacred.
Done and used.
It is silent,
Filled with holes.
Appreciated only
By Inspiration's light
Pouring through,
Behind, and around it.
The inverse shower
Upward precious.
Meets heaven's tears of grief,
Mingled with reunion's joy.
Yet, the muscle vessel
Remains unsatisfied.
Now at peace,
Its gift of hope
To be seen left behind.

TEARS ON THRONED STEPS

My eyes pour out
The pain of my heart.
Each one
With an inscription
Of words.
Words spoken
By the tongues of bearers,
Who themselves would,
If they heard,
Be heartbroken.
I cry out the heart to
Whom my soul
Is bought and knit.
Each tear
Of words received shut.
Encapsulated with gates
Of finality and unforgiveness.
The sound, as they hit
The steps of stone,
Indescribable.
Such a sad, sad knell
Of cold and hollow ring.
Tears of hope,
Then tears

From much further in,
Create a refrain of plea.
A song of reconciliation,
To rise above motives
Misjudged and unbelieved.
Each drop a prayer
Like rain of heaven's gems shower
At heaven's Lordly feet.
My tears, a mess,
On throned steps.
For Him
In His bottle
To collect.
Whose heat of anger
To scorch, I hope:
Gossip, lies, and deceit.
And to shower
Those whom I love
Yet no longer knowing,
Redemptive time.
How long yet unknown,
Because we shall share
Eternal life.

TRAVELER'S POEM

There's just quiet.
Then, change rustles gently
Through the lives besides.
Like winds sweeping,
Leaving invisible impressions
In the grasses.
Change and its course—
What was once in fellowship,
Direction parts.
After the wind—
Silence, stillness,
Amplifies that which was dearest.
No more,
Yet immortal—
Countless memories.
Time
Inevitably cannot stall,
But each traveler's heart
Travels engraved
With the friendship
That was breathed.

HEART OF SPRING

Poems turn to songs
As dirt buries the dreams
Of my past.
Creator holds the cards,
Each one with a face.
A tear for every card
I remember caused
Such unknown pain.
Omniscient peace and comfort
Takes my heart
Within His hands.
Squeezes my soul
To His heavenly bosom,
Where I am not numb,
Yet feel no pain.
The tears,
Like blood to sunshine.
There is no door.
None that I see.
Just a brand new path
I feel underneath my feet.
It's nice.
It's new.
My eyes have sunshine.

No tears.
Anything.
Adventure unknown
Can happen.
No barren land.
Everything new.
Possibilities endless
To my heart's eyes renewed.
Praise and thanks
Taste sweet on my tongue,
To the One.
No longer muddied,
My shoulders unslumped,
My arms much more limber,
I skip and I hum.
Language pours forth
In quiet, wonderful prayer
That is joy to my Savior's
Sweet ears to hear.
My eyes dart and pan
To each new thing.
On this bright, new path—
A heart's season of Spring
At long, long last.

THE MOON ROSE

The moon arose
Upon the moon rose
Of deep, crimson violet,
With beams
Of soft, white hue.
In the setting
Of the golden season
The crickets trilled
Of what she longed,
And the breath of evening
Added its chorus word of
"soon."
To blossom
For the lordly pearl,
Where moonlight and petals meet.
The night to bless,
Love shall bless,
Hence more
Sparkling, scented sweet.

GATE OF LOVE

At the gate of love,
That to step beyond,
One must hand over
The sacred,
The precious, wondrous,
To silence's key to keep.
Great and tall are its pillars,
Grand its proportions,
Even greater
Its guarded lands—
Both daunting and a comfort.
Solid and unmoving
In its stand.
The person who dares to enter
Must fight the fear,
Of after entering,
That they,
Or the heart pursued,
Might disappear.
Standing at
The gate of love,
Where offering
Is spoken and sung,
Gives pause to the called
On the threshold of admiration.

SKY IN THE NIGHT

Two stars rise,
Enveloped and cloaked
In their dance.
Two hearts throb,
In the soft and brilliant blaze,
As love's light touches,
The night sky:
Veils the heavenly,
Veils fire,
Veils the fire of their minds,
Veils the dance of stars.
As their dance sings,
They dance,
They sway,
They dip.
She sidles some steps away,
He extends his heart glow.
Knowing her feet
Are not truly going.
They twirl and rise and fall.
Starlit brilliance.
Starlight proximity.
Starlit wonder,
Shine meaning, delight, and beauty.

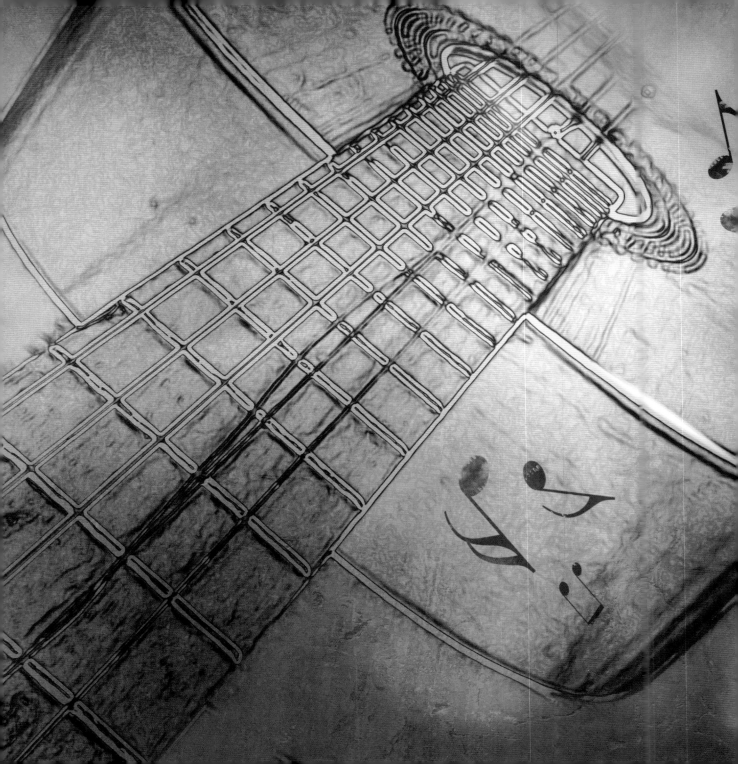

MUSICAL LOVE

His heart played
The bridges of the strings.
His eyes of ocean
Silently sang
A dream and a wish.
What it would be
To share a kiss,
Slow and sweet and long.
The guitars of our souls
Danced over the frets
Of a wooden street.
Our voices sang
Sitting midst the people
A song where we both
For impromtu concert sensed
Joy invisibly round us dancing.
Kissed by the surf.
Another evening fell.
Romance's chords amplified.
Held each other's bodies.
Hearts vibrating intertwined.
Lost to the melody
That knew no time.

LANGUAGE OF THE WIND

The language of the wind—
Few hear its voice.
Distinguish friendliness
From fierceness, not nice.
A voice unseen,
Sometimes carrying hope,
Sometimes dreams,
A voice of things to come,
So few familiar with.
Unseen vocabulary,
Yet for those
Who hear the wind
Inside their hearts,
They smile.
Time goes by.

Sometimes it comes,
Quiet and gentle,
Playing through the trees,
Speaking so protectively.
Sometimes it comes
As a torrent, a challenge—
To test a heart's life,
To scream.
Still other times it whispers,
Just above or beyond,
Of things we wish so presently,
And leaves us wondering
When promises will come to be.
But the voice of the wind
Is as faithful.

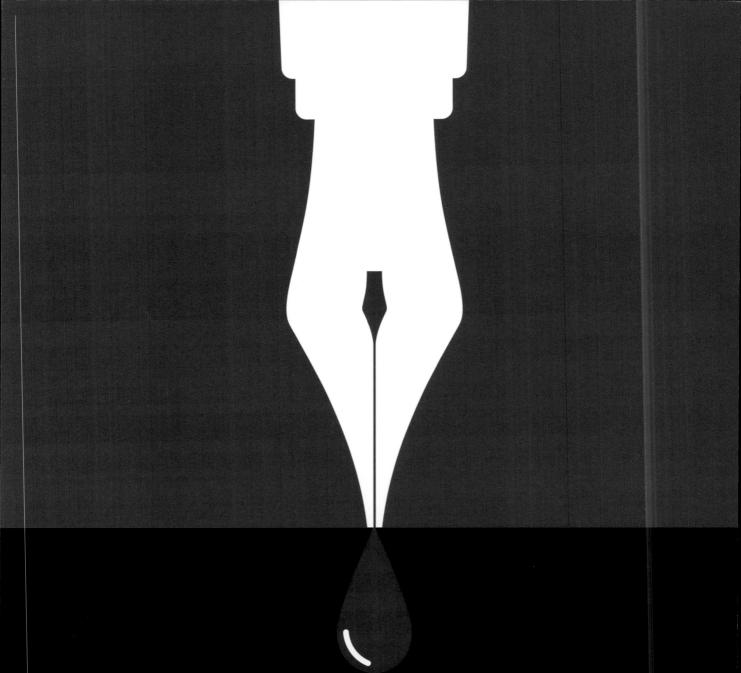

A HEART OF INK

I have written of the poet's sea.
I have writ of lover's fees.
I have writ of visions
In hues unknown to flesh.
I have writ such things
From one tiny desk.
Words poured out in liquid tears
Gathered by Heaven's hand so near.
While other's blood is red,
My blood is spectrum's pigments—
On parchment do I scratch and bleed.
Soaking in the gift from trees.
Dancing from the quill nib
Learning cursive grace
My collection so fluid,
My heart of ink
Encased in the pen
Held and forged by
Author's mighty hand.

ABOUT THE AUTHOR

Coral Tulle Hahn grew up in Maryland, enjoying Marty Stougher's "Wild America," and Jeff Corwin, Crocodile Hunter—enthralled to learn of the creatures and environment locally. She was encouraged to become involved in drawing, expressive reading, and story development and production.

In high school and onward, Coral encountered Native American Christians who explained the challenges of being a Christian. After her third college year, she moved to California to be a missionary artist for thirteen years. She also received training in film school for six years as a producer for the blossoming Eternalfeatherfilm.com.